One Surviving Poem

Forty-two poets select the one poem they would like to survive them

Edited by Howard Firkin

in case of emergency press

We are proud to acknowledge the Traditional Owners of country throughout Australia and to recognise their continuing connection to land, waters, and culture.

We pay our respects to their Elders past, present, and emerging.

We support recognition, reconciliation, and reparation.

One Surviving Poem

Forty-two poets select the one poem they would like to survive them

edited by Howard Firkin

in case of emergency press
http://www.icoe.com.au
Travancore, Victoria
Australia

Published by in case of emergency press 2019

Copyright © edited by Howard Firkin 2019

All rights reserved. Without limiting the rights under copyright reserved above, no part of this publication may be reproduced, stored in or introduced into a database and retrieval system or transmitted in any form or any means (electronic, mechanical, photocopying, recording or otherwise) without the prior written permission of both the owner of copyright and the above publishers.

ISBN 978-0-9943525-6-9

I will create a new language
Melding the modern idiom
with relics of ancient human art
It's the perfect solution to the task
of depicting my rebel logic
I should have thought of it years ago

Chris Reid

Table of contents

Introduction	v
it's all relative *Geoffrey Aitken*	7
Music isn't about standing still and being safe *Bill Cushing*	9
Nothing happens in the burbs *Anne Casey*	14
Kiss Me, Again, Again, and Again *David Estringel*	17
Luna at Dawn *Martha Patterson*	19
In my boudoir *Sofia Chapman*	21
Large and Small *Brenton Cox*	23
Windfall *Dorothy Swoope*	25
Beyond Us *S. E. Street*	27
Missing *Mary Pomfret*	30
A Christmas Poem on Mirtazapine *Em König*	32
Jazz *Joan McNerney*	34
Memorial Triptych for Three Wars *J. R. McRae*	37
Famine on the Plenty *Denise Parker*	44
Age Sixteen *Carolyn Abbs*	47
Résumé *Ursula Beaumont*	50
The Tale of Two Holes *David L. Hume*	52
Ode to lighthouses *Naida Mujkić*	65
Underpass *Alex Dreppec*	67
The Column *Dina Kafiris*	69
Time Travellers *Nalini Priyadarshni*	72
collecting apples *Carl Walsh*	75
Amity Poem *Joyce Parkes*	77
Half-sisters *David Lloyd*	79
from Surplus: An Epic *Janis Butler Holm*	81
Thinking of you *Alessandra Salisbury*	83
The Nun and the Assassin *C. A. Broadribb*	89
wonderland (in only 4 days) *Olivia De Zilva*	92
Mr & Mrs Jack-in-the-Box *Dianne Cikusa*	96
My Dream Mother *Beth Spencer*	98
Ricochet *Bree Alexander*	100
There is more *Gavin Mndawe*	102
i follow the silent road *banjo weatherald*	105
Superseding Professor Weilgart *Chris Reid*	107

to let go *Kelsi Rose*	110
Perkins Island *Rees Campbell*	113
Rights of the Child *Rhonda W. Rice*	115
Rheumatic Pain Stiffens the Spine *Kristian Patruno*	117
Poltergeist Clown *Roger Vickery*	120
Jesucristo Santifícanos *María J. Estrada*	123
The Everyday Artist and the Everlasting Muse *Michael Leach*	126
The Great Depression *Tim Hawkins*	128

Introduction

This anthology arose out of an unremarkable conversation between poets where it was noted with surprise that each of the poets present had personal favourites that had never been published. Other poems, less ambitious, less adventurous, less interesting had always been selected by editors in preference. This may tell us nothing more than poets are their own worst critics (which is unlikely to surprise anyone), but it struck me that it might be worthwhile allowing poets to present their most cherished pieces for inclusion in a single anthology.

The resulting collection is presented here and is notable for its variety.

Some of the poems are intensely personal and reflect intense moments and relationships: David Estringel's *Kiss Me, Again, Again, and Again*, Alessandra Salisbury's *Thinking of you*, Olivia De Zilva's *wonderland (in only 4 days)*. Some of the poems are reflections of the poet's place in the physical world: Rees Campbell's *Perkins Island*, Dorothy Swoope's *Windfall*, Carl Walsh's *collecting apples*. Some poems focus on family: Nalini Priyadarshni's *Time Travellers*, David Lloyd's *Half-sisters*, S. E. Street's *Beyond Us*. Other poems offer a metaphysical perspective of our lives: Geoffrey Aitken's *it's all relative*; or present the seemingly eternal political and social justice issues we confront: Kelsi Rose's *to let go*, María J. Estrada's *Jesucristo Santifícanos*. There are many poems which display a playful light-heartedness, a joy in poetry and language, and a sharp eye for comic circumstance: Em König's *A Christmas Poem on Mirtazapine*, banjo weatherall's *i follow the silent road*, the extract from Janis Butler Holm's *Surplus: An Epic*. There are simple poems and complex poems. Long and short. If I fail to find a unifying theme in the collection, I can only plead indifference: I never hoped to.

Selecting the order of poems in a collection is always a difficult chore. I struggled with the best way to present the poems, and, in the grand tradition of poets everywhere, I gave up and moved on to something more interesting. The order of the poems was determined by a process very like throwing them all up into the air and seeing how they fell. I trust you approve, but can't say I really care. I do hope, however, you enjoy the collection. I hope you rejoice in its variety and vitality. I hope you are encouraged to seek out other works by the poets included here.

Howard Firkin

it's all relative

Geoffrey Aitken

Geoffrey Aitken is a retired former Senior English teacher who is more a voice than a poet. That voice has been developed to raise issues those without cannot express. He writes to read at local 'open mic' (since 2015) and loves people and poetry equally. He was selected as one of three contributors to Friendly Street Poets' "*New Poets 19*" Anthology in 2018 which has led to 'emerging poet' status, an acknowledgement he cherishes. He is gaining some momentum with publishers who are slowly employing his reasoned articulations. Time teaching in Public Education in central Australia for thirty years, including vocational training experiences with Indigenous adults in remote communities, has irreversibly shaped his thinking. He believes maturity does not ensure wisdom.

Recent publication highlights:

"*Right Now*" (Human Rights in Australia website) has published '**for others**' and will publish '**arrhythmic**'; May & September 2019

"*Underground Press*" will publish '**crank encased**' in *Underground Zine* Issue #27 – 2019

"*Accounting, Auditing and Accountability Journal*" has accepted '**3 x workplace poems**' for publication September 2019

Adelaide Friendly Street Poets "*New Poets 19 Anthology*" - 2018 (38 poems), "*Dream-Water Fragment*" Anthology 42 - 2018 (2 poems) and "*Alchemy*" Anthology 43 - 2019 (2 poems).

Geoffrey's website: ***https://www.poetryfeasting.com/***

it's all relative

it's old
before it reaches me
i'm told

the light
the day
the news
the conversation

there's warmth though
and daylight hours are favourable
still dealing a life force
measured sometimes in moments

and so
i make the fickleness last
etch notes in my journal
ignore life's frailty
expand the impermanence
until i have possessed
the full day
calling it mine

as if it were mine to own

Music isn't about standing still and being safe

Bill Cushing

Bill Cushing has lived in Virginia, New York, Pennsylvania, Missouri, Florida, Maryland, the Virgin Islands, and Puerto Rico before moving to California. As an undergrad, he was called the "blue collar" poet by classmates at the University of Central Florida because of his years serving in the Navy and later working as an electrician on oil tankers, naval vessels, and fishing boats. He earned an MFA in writing from Goddard College in Vermont and taught for over 20 years at East Los Angeles and Mt. San Antonio colleges. He now resides in Glendale with his wife and their son.

His poetry has appeared in numerous journals, both in print and online, including *Avocet*, *Brownstone Review*, *Glomag*, *Mayo Review*, *Penumbra*, *Poetry Nook*, *Spectrum*, *The Song Is...*, and *West Trade Review*. In 2017, he was named as one of the Top Ten Poets of LA, and in 2018 he was named one of the "ten poets to watch" in Los Angeles by Spectrum publishing. In 2019, his chapbook **Music Speaks** won the San Fernando Valley National Poetry Month competition.

Bill's book, **A Formal Life**, was released in June 2019 by Finishing Line Press and is available on Amazon. It contains the following poem, which was first featured in the award-winning anthology Stories of Music, vol. 1 and was later nominated for both a Pushcart and Best of the Net award.

Bill's work can also be found at *PoemHunter.com* and *The Ekphrastic Review*.

When not writing, Bill facilitates a writing group in Eagle Rock, California (9 Bridges). He also performs with a musician in a project called "Notes and Letters" and invites anyone interested to visit and like their Facebook page:
https://www.facebook.com/groups/100185423723709/
or check their youtube page:
https://www.youtube.com/channel/UCcBq6xyF20DFZNuqaM_1x6Q

"Music isn't about standing still and being safe"

— **Miles Davis** (1926-1991)

listen

two weeks after you died
a quarter-million thronged
by the St. Johns River
to hear the music you had spawned
hoping to see you
but
even in death
you never looked back

they were all there
      Hannibal   Bird
      Chick   Jo-Jo
      Red   Jaco
      Bean   Dizzy
      my favourite Freddie Freeloader

isolated
you
were a beacon
      a flagship for messages
            of the heart

back to the crowd   unbowed

that proud dance-walk
announced by muted horn
that spoke
and broke
through all the bull
and told us about a place

Miles

ahead of everyone else
you spent a lifetime
      thinking for yourself
      speaking to every generation
playing it all:
      jazz   blues
      funk   rock
      fusion
categories took
a backseat
to creativity
      and rhythm

    space

      and feeling
           spirit

I remember fourth grade
picking up a horn
then laying it down
rock and roll was my world

what did I know

seven years later I heard

it was in the Garden
where you brought me back
to music

I walked all the way home

Miles

from that train station
my head pounding with sounds
frantic-fast as the subway
I spent the night on
        those African rhythms
        you used decades
        before anyone else
        even thought to
filling my head
letting me know
I'd have it all down cold
if I could walk
as cool as the notes you heard
        coming from

Miles

you had that thing
        that style

that spark that was
a blue flame
        jumping
        off a gas stove
igniting everything   everywhere
touching the genetic
resonant
frequency
in all

Nothing happens in the burbs

Anne Casey

A journalist/editor, media/communications director and legal author for 25+ years, Anne Casey is author of **where the lost things go** (Salmon Poetry 2017, 2nd ed 2018) and **out of emptied cups** (Salmon Poetry 2019).

She is Senior Poetry Editor of Swinburne University Melbourne's two literary journals and has won/shortlisted for poetry awards in Ireland, the USA, the UK, Canada and Australia.

Her poems have been published in *The Irish Times*, *The Canberra Times*, *Entropy*, *apt*, *Murmur House*, *Quiddity*, *Cordite*, *Verity La*, *Plumwood Mountain*, *The Incubator*, *The Honest Ulsterman*, *Stony Thursday Book*, *Into the Void*, *Autonomy anthology*, *FourXFour* (Poetry Northern Ireland) and *Burning House Press*, among others.

Nothing happens in the burbs

we lay in bed talking about nothing
till two came stomping up the stairs
raging on about nothing
one hot on his heels
what did you do to him?
nothing!

after breakfast you put music on
Adele, Sam Cooke, Joe Cocker, Emilie Sande
they had nothing in common
but us
eleven a.m. on a Saturday
dancing barefoot in the kitchen
pretending there was nothing
going on

i lolled between one and two
while you did nothing in the garden
got two's help to move it to the garage
nothing in the fridge so we cobbled something together
nothing on tv so we watched an expert panel
arguing vehemently about nothing the government
was doing nothing about while we shook our heads
knowing nothing
would change

slouching on the couch
nothing between us

but the dog
eight feet in the air
a howl and crash from upstairs
what happened??!
Nothing!! In unison, too quick
what was that all about? Nothing at all

we split a cider
yours straight from the bottle
mine from a champagne flute
making an occasion out of nothing
till we went to bed, in no hurry
we had nothing on

and there is nothing, absolutely nothing
i would change

Kiss Me, Again, Again, and Again

David Estringel

David Estringel is poet and writer of fiction, creative non-fiction, & essays. His work has been accepted and/or published by *Specter Magazine, Literary Juice, Foliate Oak Magazine, Terror House Magazine, Expat Press, 50 Haikus, littledeathlit, Down in the Dirt Magazine, Route 7 Review, Setu Bilingual Journal, Paper Trains Literary Journal, The Elixir Magazine, Soft Cartel, Harbinger Asylum, Briars Lit, Open Arts Forum, Cajun Mutt Press, Former People Journal, The Ugly Writers, Writ in Dust, Cephalopress, Twist in Time, Merak Magazine, Salt Water Soul, Cherry House Press, Subterranean Blue Poetry, Printed Words, Sunflower Sutras, Tulip Tree Publishing, Salt Ink, PPP Ezine, Digging through the Fat, Haiku Journal, Foxhole Magazine, The Basil O'Flaherty, Three Line Poetry, Agony Opera, Siren's Call Ezine, Alien Buddha Press, Synchronized Chaos, Pantheon of Poesy, The @baffled Haiku Daily, Blood Moon Rising Magazine, The Blue Nib, Fishbowl Press, Horror Sleaze Trash, Rigorous Magazine, Corvus Review, Spillwords.com, Proletaria Journal, Cherry Magazine, Bleached Butterfly, Poetry Pea (Haiku Pea), Sub Rosa Zine, TL;DR Press, Spit Poet Zine, Arthut, ICOE Press, Logos, Z Publishing, Outcast Magazine, Ponder Savant, Impspired Magazine, Drunk Monkeys, Poetizer, Channillo,* and *The Good Men Project.*

He is currently a Contributing Editor (fiction) at *Red Fez*, an editor/writer/Artist in Residence at *The Elixir Magazine*, fiction reader at *riverSedge*, Poetry Editor at *Fishbowl Press*, Artist in Residence at *Cajun Mutt Press*, and columnist at *Channillo.*

David's first book of poetry and prose **Indelible Fingerprints** was published by *Alien Buddha Press*, April 2019.

David can be found on Twitter (@The_Booky_Man) and his website at ***http://davidaestringel.com***.

Kiss Me, Again, Again, and Again

The coppery taste of meat beneath your sweet breath lingers
like a penny on the tip of my tongue.
Heads or tails?
Can't lose—
Lucky me.
My equilibrium's fucked raw,
as my hands drink in the warm curvature of your hips.
O, glorious spit—
a little dab will do ya—
streaked red and hot,
never take me from this place,
leaving me
haunted by the ghost of that breath—
your Heaven,
your Hell—
that leaves me…
quivering.
Words can't capture what's smeared on this cheek
by fingers,
sticky and sweet—
so why try?
Kiss me,
again,
again,
and again,
in that white muslin dress of thigh-stretched daisies
that roll and grin like morning shadows,
smiling at secrets hidden in dark places.

Luna at Dawn

Martha Patterson

Martha Patterson is a poet, playwright, essayist, and fiction writer. She is influenced by Emily Dickinson and the East Indian poet Rumi. Her plays have been produced in nineteen states and eight countries. Her writing has been published by *Smith & Kraus / Applause Theatre & Cinema Books*, *Pioneer Drama Service*, the *Sheepshead Review* (Univ. of Wisconsin), the *Afro-Hispanic Review*, *Silver Birch Press*, *Original Works Publishing*, *Drama Notebook*, and the *Pointed Circle* journal (Portland Community College).

Martha has two degrees in Theatre: one from Mount Holyoke College; one from Emerson College. She lives in Boston, Massachusetts.

Her website is *http://www.marthapatterson.org* and her blogspot is *http://marthapatterson.blogspot.com.*

Her books may be found on Amazon at:

https://www.amazon.com/author/marthabpatterson.

Luna at Dawn

A luna moth,
Green like the cloth of my new dress that Grandma mended
When I was five, after a classmate bit holes in it,
Appeared on my window.

Tender as a gingko leaf,
It seemed asleep on the glass
And I knew how uncommon it was to witness this,
Most especially after waking from a bad dream.

In my boudoir

Sofia Chapman

Sofia Chapman completed a Bachelor of Arts (Hons) in Modern Languages at the University of Tasmania before running away with the piano accordion to play on a theatre barge on the Rhône, Avignon, France.

Sofia has written and co-produced numerous plays at La Mama, Carlton, and also features in La Mama's 50th anniversary book. Sofia received the 2012 Melbourne Fringe 'Best Emerging Writer' Award for the epic 'The Four Accordionists of the Apocalypse'. Sofia's début short story, 'The Cave of Dr Cayla', written during a residency in France was published in *Gargouille Literary Journal* in 2016, and many poems have been published and performed here and there.

Sofia appeared at the Emerging Writers' Festival and the International Festival of Literature in Translation in 2012 and Poetry at Federation Square, 2013. Sofia's poem 'Villanelle: Detention Centre' appeared in *Regime 02*, W.A. and 'Nancy Nails, dominatrix' won *Australian Poetry* 'Poem of the Week', in 2013. Sofia's poem, 'A Boot Left in Wellington' appears in *n-SCRIBE* magazine issue 11, and 'Death of a Guinea Pig' in issue 13.

Sofia's 'Desperate Gallery' was performed in the SHORT and SWEET short play Festival at Seymour Centre, Sydney and the Arts Centre, Melbourne. It has also been performed in Canada, New Zealand, the United States and the UK. 'Desperate Gallery' was published by *Lazy Bee*, UK, in 2012, and is now available online at *Lazy Bee Publishing*.

Sofia is a professional accordionist with the band **Vardos**.

Discover more at *https://www.vardos.com.au/sofia.htm*

In my boudoir

In my boudoir,

a moth lies trapped

like an old flame.

I'll release you under these conditions.

Let me fly instead of you,

flit, moonlit,

on powdered wings.

Let me eat my clothes instead of you,

and no, it's not that I don't fit into them.

You doubt my defiance of gravity,

yet I don't feel fat in this

cell you light

with your presence, you

Blanche DuBois in my boudoir.

Let me eat my words instead of y

Large and Small

Brenton Cox

Brenton Cox is a 52-year-old man who lives happily in Adelaide, Australia. He currently works as a consultant to not-for-profit organisations and charities and specialises in the areas of governance, financial management and start-ups. He has a particular interest in working life and how it interacts with personal spirituality.

Brenton is a published writer and poet and enjoys reading non-fiction, travelling and spending excessive amounts of time at cafes. His first book, **The Suburban Mystic**, is currently in the throws of being published. It is a work of non-fiction and through a combination of poetry and prose, it explores the vagaries of what it means to live a mystical life in the suburbs.

Brenton can be contacted at *bcconsulting111@gmail.com*.

Large and Small

You are the small
in the large.
A drop in the ocean,
a cloud in the sky,
a detail in the story.
You live in the shadow
of the grand expanse.

You are the large
in the small.
The ocean in a drop,
the sky in a cloud,
the story in a detail.
You live as the shadow
of the grand expanse.

Windfall

Dorothy Swoope

Dorothy Swoope is an award-winning poet. Her writings are published internationally in print and online. She is the author of two poetry publications: **Ice Dancing** and **Contemplating the View**; a chapbook: **The Touch of a Word**; and her childhood memoir: **Wait 'til Your Father Gets Home!**

In her former life she was a librarian and pre-school educator. She emigrated from the USA and now resides on the South Coast of New South Wales. When not weaving words with nature, she is weaving upcycled materials.

Windfall

Collecting windfall wood
in the sun still afternoon
belonging to bird song
and swirling motes of insects
spiralling in the shafts of light
beaming through the trees.

These sticks released
from their battered crowns
after bitingly cold winds
a week's worth of kindling
broken and bulging
fill my willow basket.

Absorbed by sunshine and sweet singing
and silent whirling winged things
I linger
feeling like a rock
solid and settled
without thought or desire
the earth humming beneath me.

Beyond Us

S. E. Street

S.E. Street's fiction, nonfiction and poetry have been published in the UK, Canada, United States, Australia, and New Zealand. She is the recipient of the Dymocks Short Story Prize for fiction, the Hunter Writers Award and is the South Coast Writers Centre HARP winner for poetry.

Beyond Us

As I drove down the valley,
my father was silent beside me.
His head moved deliberately.
I knew what he was doing.
His photographer's eye was framing
the distant mountains,
paled overnight by early snow.
The medley of the autumn trees:
conifers, alders, sycamores.
The stands of silver birch
against a peacock sky.
He lingered on the width of the glacier-fed river—
the milky turquoise channel of swollen current,
the pebbled shoals so clear and clean,
drinkable, in the morning sunlight.
The valley's triumphant showiness seemed almost cruel.
This is not the last time you will see this,
I almost said, as he gathered the images
like a squirrel storing nuts for the winter.
We will be back. Next year.

With his thumb, he pointed over his shoulder
to a clearing, carved like the seat of a chair
in the side of a peak, reminding me
of where to watch the sunsets.
I opened my window a fraction
to let my melancholy escape.
Cold air blasted my ear.

We bemoaned the long stops
on our childhood car trips
while our father painstakingly
composed a photograph.
Wordlessly, he led us to perceive
the significance of the world
outside the grandeur of ourselves.

Standing in the clearing,
I am dwarfed by the encircling mountains.
The sun trails a farewell hand above a ridge,
a gold fingered salute to the day.
The valley's shadows smudge into darkness
and the stars, undiminished by city lights,
spawn luxuriantly beyond the rim of the horizon.

Missing

Mary Pomfret

Mary Pomfret is a poet and writer who lives and works in Central Victoria. Her poems have been published widely and in 2016 her chapbook **'Fractures and Other Thin Confusions'** was published by Picaro Poets. The poem *Missing* has been published in "Tamba Literary Journal" and is also featured in her collection **"Writing in Virginia's Shadow"**, Ginninderra Press, 2013. Mary draws her inspiration from life and believes that there is nothing so terrible that it can't be hallowed and transformed into art. La Trobe University awarded Mary a PhD doctorate for her creative work in 2016.

Email: *marywriter@live.com*

Website: *www.marypomfret.com*

Facebook: Mary Pomfret Author

Missing

Today I missed you. I missed you yesterday too, but today I missed you more. I'm not sure why. Maybe it was because it was raining. Early this morning the sun was shining but then it clouded over and started to drizzle. The soft misty rain continued for most of the day. It stopped for a short time around mid-day, so I went to sit in the garden under the autumn tree and ate my cheese sandwich. But just as I finished eating, it started to rain softly, and softly rain so I went back inside and stared out the window for a while. I listened to my new Nick Cave CD. I played it three times and then I decided to take my dog for a walk. The air outside smelled fresh and the rain on my face mixed with tears of missing you. Some days I miss you more than others — it's hard to know why that is really. Missing you is a hard thing to quantify. I guess it's just that some days ache more than others. Later, when I came back from my walk I played Nick Cave again. The phone rang once and for some reason I thought it might be you, but of course it wasn't. It was still raining softly and softly raining at tea time, but it didn't matter because I wasn't going out anywhere. I decided to skip dinner and sat down and watched the news and the weather report. Apparently it will be raining again tomorrow and the next day and the day after that.

Today I missed you. And I will miss you tomorrow, and all the days after that and all the days after that...

A Christmas Poem on Mirtazapine

Em König

Em König is a multidisciplinary artist living and working on stolen Kaurna land.

His poetry can be found in *Meniscus, Cordite, SWAMP, On Dit, Pink Cover, Malevolent Soap*, in closets, under floorboards and drowning in the rising oceans. His debut chapbook, '**Lightly, on the Skin**', was released in 2018 by in case of emergency press and his first full-length collection of poetry will be released by Cordite Books in 2020.

Em is one half of music/performance duo GIRL who exist as both a touring band and as makers of immersive, sound-based performance works. Their latest performance 'Masc', which explores the complexities and intersections of toxic masculinities and queerness, is in development throughout 2019 and their debut album of the same name will be released soon.

Em is also currently completing a PhD in creative writing at the University of Adelaide.

Other interests include PJ Harvey, RuPaul's Drag Race, gardening and popular cosmology.

www.emkoenig.com
www.girl-official.com

A Christmas Poem on Mirtazapine

Heavy is the burden of an unwanted pair
of socks, and we carry this through, always
into the following year. But in spite of charity
and Jesus I fucking hate Christmas
and these are simply the reasons:
1. Babies playing with boxes instead of dolls.
2. Fresh torn tree-pattern paper.
3. The smell is nothing like a fir.
4. My uncle's fist up a dead bird's arse.
5. I no longer eat butter or flesh.
6. Shortening.
7. Do not act upon your urges.
8. There is truly nothing wrong with speaking.
9. They is plural.
10. It will be 40 degrees again.
11. My nephew will not look at me.
12. I do not want him to.
13. What is it you actually do, again?
       I do like the sweets though and stick
       some in my purse for later. They will taste
       like metal and like every other year
       we will be judged for leaving early.
       Butterless, stockinged—an uncle
       or something like it.

Jazz

Joan McNerney

Joan McNerney's poetry has appeared in more than seven hundred publications in over thirty countries, both online and in print. She has been nominated four times for Best of the Net. Her books have been published by fine small literary presses and she also has e-book titles:
Love Poems for Michael
http://booksonblog5.blogspot.com
when the moon is new
https://issuu.com/fowlpoxpress/docs/finalcopywhenbook_2fabdb37849d2e

She has performed readings broadcast on numerous public radio and television stations. She has recited her poetry at the National Arts Club, Gramercy Park, New York City, State University of New York, Oneonta, State University of Texas, Houston, McNay Art Institute, San Antonio, and other distinguished venues. The American Academy of Poetry sponsored a personal appearance at Bright Hills Art Gallery in New York.

Joan lives in the northeast USA.

Her latest title is **The Muse in Miniature** available now on both amazon.com and cyberwit.net.

Jazz

the kitchen sits
in fruit soup...
steamed apricot
mango shadow

down thru spinning
smoke into hot light
blink beat

body ends dangle
lead eye skin cement
high on tongue

night pasted among
buildings Styrofoam clouds
moon hung beneath billboard

rolling pass wet
rocked streets
soul tramp
diamond panhandlers watch
paper birds slices of
the daily news drift in air

comes cool ether
whispers up door
climbing dusty corridor

tree windows lapping lisp
door slams again noise again
then none void nothing syncopates
noise again door slams tree bare frozen

caught in the image of 7 candles
within 7 candles flames of air
7 light bulbs growing out of each other
7 silver circles coined from 7 silver rings

clear as blazing sheets
of glass yet
vague as dust
an ice cube on wood table
in front of crushed velvet
    melt
    poured
    peeled

when this sky now boiling with
stars is strapped black
in pinched air thru sucked mind
swimming pass spaced time
will be one silent
note up.

Memorial Triptych for Three Wars

J. R. McRae

J.R. Poulter/J.R. McRae has been published in Australia, the USA, India and elsewhere and has won awards for her poetry in Australia and India and awards for her fiction books for adults and for children in Australia and the USA. J.R. has written ever since she could hold a pen; it's a life habit! Her children have grown and flown—she now lives with her husband and the young rescue cat she adopted.

- Four poems included in the collection of War Memorial, Canberra, 2018
- International Poetry Award, The Great Indian Poetry Contest 2018
- Judge, Week 7 Poetry Challenge, On Fire Cultural Movement, India
- Gold Medal, Illustration Award, Readers' Favorite, 2018
- Panelist—Poetry's importance to children and in education, QPF 2017
- Panelist—Publishers' Panel, Story Arts Festival of Children's Literature, 2017

Awards

Children's Choice, New Zealand

Top Ten Children's Books & YA Books, New Zealand,

"Mending Lucille" won Crichton, CBCA Award

Premier's Recommended Reading List, NSW, Australia

Poetry—Premier's Open Literature Award [Warana]

Simone Wood Award, USA

LiFE Award, Literature for Environment

Award-Winning Finalist, International Book Awards

Winner, Purple Dragonfly Award—Picture Books, 5 years and younger

"Getting Home" Winner, Purple Dragonfly Award—Best Illustrations

Readers' Favorite International Book Award Winner

Websites

www.jenniferrpoulter.weebly.com

http://jrmcrae-subversive.weebly.com

Word Wings Publishing *http://www.lulu.com/spotlight/wordwings*

Word Wings on Facebook

Instagram: word_wings_books

Memorial Triptych for Three Wars

Panel I. And Old Men Remember

In the brooding dark we are
Just ordinary men remembering
Loved ones left, fields fallow, idle dogs
And chores undone.
We are alone with thoughts we cannot let the morning see.
We wait.
Those for whom death's become habit, sleep.
Sentries hold the night on a knife edge.
We wait, listening for the breathing of the man alongside
Intent on the cold light from gun barrel and bayonet—
A flash of eyes—just checking
Battlelines drawn in furrowed brows.

The sun is raised from the smelting ground of earth—
First light soaks red the long horizon,
Seeps down between our fingers,
Fires minds and forges spirits that waiting kills—
Memories ricochet off the deadly mundanities
Of another entrenched day.

In the brooding darkness we are
Just ordinary men remembering
Compatriots gone—spirit and earth burdened with
The awful familiarity of death—
We are alone with thoughts the morning outlines harsh and clear—
We listen for the breathing of old mates,

Light catches on medals burnished with angst –
A flash of eyes—
Knowing the glint of salt on corroded cheeks.

The thunder is distant—
The far noise of highways for the soul
And the vast tracts of no man's land
Where death cries long into the after night.
In the dark we walked the fine line
Between yesterday and tomorrow,
The invisible line where enemies become
Just ordinary men—
Remembering—

Memorial Triptych for Three Wars J. R. McRae

Part II. Golgotha—The Place of the Skull

They holed up in caves mouthing the silence
Crying up from the ground—
Cold rations and cold bed,
Damp from the sweat of earth and the dew of fear,
Strangers sharing—who never knew the forest,
Whose eyes swept plains or skyscapes seared with buildings—
Whose vision's narrowed to the sight of a gun.
There is an expectation—
After the first rush of bravado is survived—
And a reckoning,
A life for a life, kill or be killed,
That's all.

They wait—young men with sweethearts, older men with families,
Boys with stubble on their chins—
Just grateful for an accepting cave to shelter from the dark.
First light they come clear of the forest,
Trees thinned to a barbed wire fence, warning with its crown of thorns,
"Enter. Tie this around your heart,
Lacerate till it can no longer bleed,
Bind it tight around your head till your eyes burst with seeing."

The quiet was unsettling—
Where were the men in worn fatigues,
Comrades in arms to laugh with and embrace,
To make the sacrifice sane.
The men held their breath,
Withdrew into the caverns of their own eyes
And edged forward.

The eldest of them rolled the stone from the door—
Slowly they recognised the truth the dark concealed—
Stared, blinked, turned desperate to disclaim
The depths within the cavernous heart,
Only to meet with eyes honed into rock
Penetrating beyond the brink of self to cry,
"Though a man lay down his life for a friend,
Both must bleed
For Cain, still walking
Where Abel's blood cries out."

Memorial Triptych for Three Wars J. R. McRae

Part III. Celluloid Screaming

Syncopated war with napalm, the 1812 overture and strangers
Shooting celluloid at men
With mud splashed minds and bloodied hands—
Screaming at each other in unison—
For sanity's sake.

Praying peasants watch helpless everything burn.
There are no candles can be lit against this god—
The career soldier who has learned
Not to tally the price he puts on life and shies
From the measuring stick held by newsreel cameramen—
Lest his woman avert her eyes from the cost of medals
Sitting heavy on his chest.

The whoop-whoop of heli-blades rape the air.
Steel-eyed birds that prey on unborn children
Cradled in peasants women's hips and the loins of men
Who never wanted to be there.
No good guys, no bad guys—
Everyone wakes screaming—
Everyone has a list of names that blur with reading—
Missing inaction   killed in action   lost—
No one reads memorials to the living dead
That signpost the authority to deny.

Tchaikovsky is eternally blasting out
The hell of drowning temple bells—
Dead silence precursors storms and nightmare reel reruns—
In foreign countries life keeps up

Cataclysmic clashing and continuing.
The reel unwinds, unwinds, unwinds relentlessly.
The nightmare is enshrined in celluloid
For sons and grandsons to wonder at, but not
The rawness at the edge of fear where gnawing rat's teeth eat and eat.
Images frozen on celluloid don't bleed—
But the scream continues, the scream continues on
And on, the screaming merges with repeats—
Everything's reduced to
Black and white.

Famine on the Plenty

Denise Parker

Denise Parker is an award-winning Queensland poet living in The Gap, a leafy suburb on the outskirts of Brisbane.

She has always enjoyed the beauty and magic of words in both English and French and has been writing poetry for a number of years.

After raising three children and enjoying a rewarding career teaching languages, she has had time to travel with her husband throughout Australia, in their caravan, 'Ultréia'. The spiritual beauty and variety of the landscapes she has encountered have inspired many of her poems.

It was during one of these trips through Outback Australia that the incident that inspired the poem, 'Famine on the Plenty', occurred.

Her poem, 'Autumn Love', was published in the '**Poetry d'Amour 2017 Anthology of Love Poems**', *www.wapoets.wordpress.com*

Notes on the text of 'Famine on the Plenty'

The Plenty Highway is a remote, long, and notoriously corrugated highway linking the Northern Territory and Boulia in Queensland.

Peter Falconio was a British tourist murdered in the Outback in 2001.

Famine on the Plenty

we saw you there
standing forlornly
bonnet up
abject mien
smoking motor

you were Black
we left you there

the road was long
reputation grim
corrugations abounded
kilometres beckoned
Falconio smouldered

you were Black
we left you there

the websites warned
we had aged, were frail
the roadside trap
the single male
the lurking doom

you were Black
we left you there

Famine on the Plenty *Denise Parker*

the Father had thundered
amplified homily
the abandoned soul
the indifferent travellers
one Good Samaritan

you were Black
we left you there

we pondered later
our conscience stricken
what could we have done
two septuagenarians
but one scar remained

you were Black
and we left You, there

Age Sixteen

Carolyn Abbs

Carolyn Abbs is a Western Australian poet published in leading journals such as *Westerly, Cordite, Rabbit, Axon: Creative Explorations, The Best Australian Poems 2014, Australian Book Review 'States of Poetry'*, and *Australian Poetry Journal*. She has a Ph.D from Murdoch University (2000) where she taught in the School of Arts for a number of years. Her poetry collection, **The Tiny Museums**, is published with UWA Publishing, 2017.

Age Sixteen

dawn sliced open   with a scalpel
stark   cold   and still
i could not   believe   in the normality of trees
              birds sang string thin

i drove in the rain: neurological terms   churning
in my brain   my gut   ask the mother   measure
the head   twitch in the eye   get her quick
               sign here   here

your shaved head   nil by mouth   i could not
tell you   how afraid i was   speed of surgical
gown   clatter   of metal on trays   brisk nurses swished
a curtain   around your bed

              in the void   i smoothed
a mask of calm on my face   told you stories   of when
you were little   i tried so hard to fold you
                    back into the past

but they came   took you   the length of corridors   i ran
alongside   caught a glimpse of white light
        and the doors swung shut   and

           i stood   with every precious second of you
pressed firmly against my heart
               for hours   and hours

they brought you back   a bald old man   sunk in white linen
      tubes   drips   oxygen
                the shock of ad hoc   medical remedies
                                        the kindness of nurses
                    midnight ticked   into the deepest dark

then
as if through the chill of snow
you spoke   like the first purple crocus of spring

Résumé

Ursula Beaumont

Ursula is a writer working from her studio on the Fleurieu Peninsula in sunny South Australia. She thoroughly enjoys sharing words and their endless combinations, the pictures they paint, the rhythms they make and the thoughts they can inspire. She likes to wallow in black text on white paper and also loves to see visual art lending a hand to picture poems.

To see more of her work, visit *www.ursulabeaumont.art*

Résumé

I'm the lively electrician
I'm the quack physician
I'm the postman's cap
I'm a dusty side-track
I'm day and dusk
I'm a subfusc husk
I'm here not there
I'm blonde not fair
I'm full-force steam
I'm your half-whipped dream
I'm a cultured pearl
I'm a Mallee burl
I'm coffee beans grinding
I'm a country road winding
I'm the fatal attack
I'm the sorry throw-back
I am polite
but an anthropophagite
I'm the neighbour's neurosis
I'm engrossed in Gnosis
I'm down one rib
and I love to fib.

The Tale of Two Holes

David L. Hume

David L. Hume lives off grid on a small homestead along a small valley somewhere in Southern Tasmania, that he shares with a dog, goats, geese, ducks, chickens and a fine woman that he dreams with and dreams with him.

He once dallied with academia, flirted with teaching and has written on art and tourism and quite a bit about ceramic art or crockery.

Now he farms, makes contraband cheese and salami and writes poems about where and how he lives, that aspire to be short stories. All of which he is happy to share.

The Tale of Two Holes

Bill's Hole and Ben's Hole

Bill woke to the rooster,
lifted the curtain
like the skirt of the day,
to see the morning fog
lighted by the low sun.

He threw the drape open
and sank back
into the warm divot
that cradled his sleep.

He watched
as the sun grew strong
and burned off the fog,
revealing its fractured shafts
through the tall trees
where his land ended.

Ben startled
to the beep
of the alarm clock,
that glowed and clanked
on the bedside table.

Restless he turned,
flapped a hand,
silenced the clock
and clicked on the bedside lamp.

He coughed,
cleared his throat,
scratched the sleep
from his eyes
and shuffled through to the en suite.

The Tale of Two Holes   *David L. Hume*

He farted,
cleared his bowels,
scratched the sweat
from his balls
and shuffled through to the kitchen.

Bill tried to ignore his bladder,
it's nagging growing more constant
and his control less reliable
as the years went on.

The sun had climbed
above the trees.
Past the frame of the bedroom window.
Bill knew it would now be lighting the kitchen.

Bearing an almost bursting stork
before him
he toddled to the back door,
took seven steps
and libated
a bountiful lemon tree.

Relieved,
he plucked two knobbly skinned fruit
and retraced his path.
The sun warmed his skin
and the wood stove his cockles.

He filled a battered coffee pot
and slid it onto the hot plate.
Squeezed two lemons
into a glass,
stirred in a pinch
of course ground chilies,
slugged it in one
and assumed a location
from where to ponder his kingdom.

Ben poured a glass
of orange coloured juice

from a plastic carton.
Flipped open the lid
of a gleaming kettle,
filled it and flicked a switch.
He scooped two teaspoons
of brown granules
into a mug with a picture
of a small related child on it
and slipped two
uniform slices
into an obese red toaster,
that matched the kettle
and dominated the kitchen bench.

The kettle popped
and the toaster pinged.
He made light brown liquid
and brown dried bread.

Bill's espresso grumbled
for his attention.
He poured a small beaker
of black pitch
and placed the pot
on the side of the stove.

He then slid a scuffed saucepan
from the edge
to the hot plate.
It's lid quickly rattled
in response
and he tipped
it's smooth white paste
into a bowl,
drizzled it with golden
grainy honey
and added a splash
of still warm milk.

The Tale of Two Holes   David L. Hume

Ben flicked on the radio,
as he chewed his toast.
He cared not for the news,
but the weather was important.

He could always predict the weather.
At least in part.
"Possible showers."
"Occasional showers."
"Isolated showers."
"Late showers."
"Early showers."

Bill scooped up porridge,
refilled his beaker
and noted the heavy dew
and clear skies.
Nice soft ground.
He thought to himself.
Better remember my hat.

He plonked a tired cloth
tie dye hat on his head.
The type that spoke of a brim
but really offered no protection
from sun or rain.

He slipped into a cracked
pair of work boots.
The type that used to be made
in the local town
and still traded as local
but were now made overseas
and aged and fell apart more quickly.

Outside
he gathered a long handled spade,
wrapping his palm
around the smooth
hardwood shaft
with a comforting caress.

And a heavy iron bar,
spike at one end
chisel blade at the other.
He felt no tenderness
for this implement.

Ben marched
across the gravel yard
to a foreboding steel barn.
Took a fat spiky set of keys
from his pocket.
Fitted one into
a fist sized padlock
and slid open a heavy door.

Placing his shiny booted foot
on the metal plated step
he hoisted himself
aboard an equally
polished green tractor,
bucket to the fore,
auger at the stern.

He traced the curve
of the wheel
with a soft plump index finger.
Then selected another key
from the spiky bunch
that prickled in his pocket
but made him feel good.

An array lit up before him.
He marvelled at its luminescence.
The beast jerked to life,
its low rumble
comforting.
He put it in gear and abruptly
set off for the row of tall trees
that defined his boundary.

The Tale of Two Holes   David L. Hume

Bill set his shovel on the pasture.
Stood on it.
It sank to the depth of the blade.
He retracted it by half
and leaned back.
He knew that the size of the blade
was beyond the capacity of his knees.

He repeated the process,
marking out a two foot circle.
Then divided the round into quarters,
before levering out the turf
in neat sections.

"Nice thick root development."
He mumbled, as he set the turf aside.
It's four quarters
reassembled
into one sod

Bill was in the habit of talking
to himself.
Indeed he spoke more to himself
than the woman he lived with.
Which, while sometimes she complained,
she was mostly grateful for.

As he was grateful
for her efforts
in the workplace,
bringing home
a wage,
that increasingly
they had little need for
and kept in a secret place
in the chook shed.

Bill repeated the process,
lifting spadefuls
of crumbly loam
into a separate pile.
"That's fine dirt that is."

He paused
to feel the texture
of the soil,
and return darkness back
to a fat writhing worm,
that had not quite escaped
the thrust of his blade,
and mumbled again.
"I wonder how vegans dig holes?"

With the twitch of a lever
Ben raised the steel auger
that dangled limply
from the rear of his machine.
And with a second twitch
set its spiral form into action.
With minimal effort
he pushed another lever
that dropped
the bore smoothly
into the earth.
One.
two,
three,
four hundred mils
it drilled into the ground.
The earth, a compound
of sod, loam,
small stones and subsoil
lifted along the spine
of the auger
and fell into one heap.

Bill reached a depth of ten inches.
He was often questioned
about his measurements,
in that passive aggressive manner
that passed for criticism today.
"Don't we use metres
and kilometres in Australia?"

The Tale of Two Holes　　　　　　　　　　　　David L. Hume

To which Bill responded
"It's my land
and I'll measure it
in links and chains if I want."

The pile of dark loam grew
until his blade struck hard
into the subsoil.
He scraped and levered
palm size rocks,
flat and round,
that at first seemed more
of a problem than eventuated.

Another pile.
Brown compacted clay,
Its sculpted angles,
like abstract cookies,
was deposited next to the loam.
Bill gathered a biscuit,
snapped it
and cast it aside.
A smaller,
shallower
cairn of excavated pebbles
completed the row.

He paused again
to examine one particular stone.
Black and elongated,
a blunted point at one end,
it fitted snugly in the palm of his hand
and his fingers fell neatly
around its form.
He set it aside.

At five hundred mils
Ben struck resistance.
He pushed harder
on the black knobbed lever.
It bounced back.

He leaned in.
It kicked back again.
He flicked two levers.
Shut down the engine.
Blew out a puff of frustration
and alighted the cab.
"Bugger" he said with a smirk,
knowing that his wife would admonish his cursing.

And knowing that she was right.
For she put the gentleman
into his farmer.
Just as she put money
into the bank,
that paid for his toys,
and everything else
that allowed him to farm.

Hands on hips
he tipped back
the cap
that came with the tractor.
He stared into the hole.
He hoped he was
but knew he wasn't
deep enough.
A gang of black cockatoos
laboured past,
mocking him in their call.

Bill had cast aside
his old ratty sweatshirt.
And his equally ratty tee shirt,
with its faded rock and roll image,
was clammy with sweat.

He'd also abandoned
the long handle spade
and was now heaving
on the bar.
This was not the first

The Tale of Two Holes David L. Hume

bar he'd heaved on
but it was the most exhausting.

Lift and drop
with thrust.
And bounce back.
Catch and repeat.
A breath of spark
arising
from the point of impact.
A tiny impression
of recent history
recorded with each drop.

Ben pondered
the idea of moving his impression
but instead booted the tractor to life,
spun it around
and dug wider.
And wider,
and wider,
and still wider.
And each time
he sought the edge,
each time
he felt the rock and jar
off the metal bucket.
At last he stopped
and cursed
and smiled
with a glance
over his shoulder.

Bill felt the twang of the bar,
as it wedged between
the two halves
of the newly cleaved rock.
"Got you,
yer fucker."

He levered it sideways.
To and fro.
Like a loose tooth
it crunched.
It wobbled,
and sucked
in the surrounding clay.

He excavated around the edges
and pried one uneven half
above the other.
Its full size revealed,
it disappointed.

The clay that harboured
the rock
turned from gritty
yellow brown
to smooth blue grey.
Reaching in
he plucked
a plug from the side.
Moist and pliable
it played like putty
between thumb
and forefinger.
He shaped a rough ball
then flattened it.
His individual mark impressed
he set it aside.

Ben dumped mouthfuls
of indistinct fill
into the ragged depression.
Pulling levers,
with syncopated rhythm,
he was at one
with his machine.

The Tale of Two Holes   *David L. Hume*

And the joy
shone on his face,
like a small boy
in a sandpit.

He patted down
the shallow mound,
pondered why
what came out
never all went back in,
and how a mark
was always left.

Then swung around
and dropped
the spinning auger.
Deep,
deep,
deeper
it bored into the ground.

He lifted,
turned
and drove on.

Bill dropped
his spade
into the hole,
and eyed the notch
on the shaft
that told him
he was deep enough.
Then, gathering his tools,
took six,
exaggerated strides,
Billometres,
to the next spot.

Ode to lighthouses

Naida Mujkić

Naida Mujkić was born in 1984. She holds PhD in Literature and she works as a docent behind the front desks at two universities in Bosnia and Herzegovina (BiH). She is a member of PEN Center BiH. She was a guest artist at Q21 Museumsquartier Wien and Goten Publishing Skopje. So far, she has published five books of poetry and one book of lyrical prose. She has participated in several international poetry and literature festivals, such as Istanbul international poetry and literature festival, 5. Gol Saatleri Şiir Akşamı, 16 . Evenings International Sapanca (Turkey), 34. Festival des migrations, des cultures et de la Citoyenneté (Luxembourg), SUR (Croatia), and many more. She has also been chosen to present her poetry at the Mediterranea 18 Young Artists Biennale (Albania).

Ode to lighthouses

The first lighthouse. Red and white stripes,
It flows off into pupils, into shadows
Of pastel dresses lifted by the wind
It empties out into tiny spaces between bystanders

There's a rock in the landscape from which
Ropes are scattering and falling on cliffs
A dandelion defying the wind
His agony captivates me.

The second lighthouse. It has its oldest
Lighthouse keeper. He's lying and I know, he
is glancing at it with his left eye. I first sprinkled the mound
With chamomile, and then with crumbled

Mimosas, and finally the fire
Came. Dark grass and iron ore rocks.
We are making longs strides on the rocks.
Where can the sea go when the lighthouses say nothing.

And false reflections.
Ships are passing, ships and hopes
Like little trees in the dark grass. I've unbuttoned
My shirt. After numbness. In front of a man who was crying.

The third lighthouse. It follows God's path
Though it's made of sand bricks. It's terrifyingly alone.
But it used to be crazy of love. And it was drawing
Houses on the ashy sky, as living proofs of himself.

Underpass

Alex Dreppec

Alex Dreppec (pen name)—born 1968 close to Frankfurt as "Alexander Deppert", studied psychology and linguistics and went to Boulder/Colorado for his Ph.D. (finished 2001). German author with hundreds of publications (both poetry and science) in German journals and anthologies, both the most renowned ("Der große Conrady"—since 2008) and the best sold among them. "Wilhelm Busch" Prize 2004.

Numerous English poems were (/will be) published on all five continents, literally, e.g. in "Cincinnati Review", "Notre Dame Review" (USA), "Orbis", "The Interpreter's House", "The Journal" (UK), Voice & Verse Poetry Magazine (Hongkong), New Contrast (South Africa).

Regular author of "Das Gedicht", the biggest poetry journal of Europe. He invented the "Science Slam", an event format where scientists present their own research work. It has spread internationally. Newest poetry book: Alex Dreppec: **"Tanze mit Raketenschuhen / Dance with Rocket Shoes"**, chiliverlag, 2016, ISBN 978-3-943292-50-3

http://www.dreppec.de/english_dreppec.html

Underpass

Unbosomed unbelief, unheard until untold
underworld's underlings unzip, unpack, unfold.
Unnumbered undertones, unbarred unconsciousness,
underachievers, unfertilized unless
under umbrellas, uprising unknowingly,
underpass underdogs unfold unguardedly.

Untamed undertow, uncovered underground:
us, untangling uncharted ultrasound.
Unheard underdog's unwanted uprightness:
unconfirmed uproar, uncashed utterly unless
under umbrellas, uprising unknowingly,
underpass underdogs unfold unguardedly.

The Column

Dina Kafiris

Born in Sydney to Greek parents, Dina Kafiris travelled to Athens at the first opportunity to study philosophy. Since then, her poetry, fiction and essays, have appeared in literary and scholarly journals in Australia and Europe, such as *American, British and Canadian Studies*, *The Journal*, *Horizon Review*, *Odyssey Magazine*, among others. She was a regular member and collaborator of the Corais group of the literary review *Nea Synteleia*, (New End of the World), under the eminent Greek poet Nanos Valaoritis. Her poetry collection **The Blinding Light Circling Elpida, in one act**, was published in 2014 by the British publisher, Original Plus, and is part of the forthcoming trilogy **21st-century Modern Greece: The First Decade**. She was a recipient of the Gladstone's Library General Scholarship Fund, and until recently, Writer in Residence and Guest Lecturer at Kingston University London.

The Column

La Torre Pendente di Pisa, failed to stand vertically.
Specialists blamed this on its poor foundation.
Her column followed a different school of thought;
a pillar whose strength rivalled that of the Pentelic marble,
yet suffered considerable damage from a playground mishap.

Unlike Frida, she picked up the pen,
employing a battalion of words,
imprints of a lost childhood, abundant phrases
feuding backbiting tongues and discourteous stares:
'A curse of the illiterate,' her mother swore.
For a while she walked on stilts, transforming flatties
to freaks in a touring sideshow;
crayons and felt tips coloured in kingdoms, distant lands
where she subdued the sanctimonious drivel of princesses,
secured the admiration of knights and kings, sentenced traitors,
consoled peasants, adhered to the teachings of ancient prophets—
here her pagan eyes were compared to flawless emeralds.
Boredom helped create a world
where she was permitted to intervene,
but even this distraction could not protect her from the fisted hand
striving on paper to bow to the one reality,
that she, like the tower, might topple.
Frequent rendezvous with Hippocrates's 'disciples' displeased her,
morning breaths unkindly met; meticulous sculptors
strapping her torso with bandages, fitting her for a bespoke corset—
the smell of drying plaster repeatedly made her gut churn.
So she shut her eyes, migrated to a self far from the common folk

where her beauty equalled Helen of Troy's and Lady Guinevere's,
reflecting on whether Waterhouse would have been as kind
as he was in his depiction of 'Circe Poisoning the Sea'.
'Beauty is only skin deep,' her father promised,
barely in school uniform
when the pointing of fingers persecuted her.
As a pupil, she walked hopeful,
having learnt that the skill of writing could make her notable.
Her scribbled notes spoke of society and the perils of women;
she refused to accept that the plight of Austen,
Woolf, Plath... went unrewarded.

Her column would be restored. Now a swan in a crowd,
she followed the gift inspired by a prolific imagination,
she crossed into the real world where she'd gaze
from the decks of ships, from port to port,
out of plane windows that carried her across
the unkempt and barren landscapes of foreign continents.
In these adopted hometowns, she would be compensated,
taken aback by the rewards bestowed upon the future:
an illustrious history of literary garlands,
accolades that firmly established her reputation
as a distinguished woman of letters.
'The pen in time forgives all,' she said at a news conference.
These words forced scholars into the donated archive
of a university library,
scavenging for truths, frustrated at their inability
to decode the wit that had eased her journey,
fictional oeuvre that served as a testimony to the stone years.

Time Travellers

Nalini Priyadarshni

Nalini Priyadarshni is a feminist, poet, writer, editor, translator, and educationist though not necessarily in that order who has authored **Doppelganger in My House** and co-authored **Lines Across Oceans** with late D. Russel Micnhimer. She is an editor at The Women Inc., a place for every woman and her expression. Her writings have appeared in numerous literary journals, podcasts and international anthologies including *The Madras Courier, Ugly Writers, The Open Road Review, Your One Phone Call, In Between Hangovers, Asian Signature, Chantarelle's Notebook, Counter Currents, Art Hut* and *Silence Between Notes.*

Nalini has edited several poetry collections including **Contemporary Major Indian Women Poets** (2016), **English Section of Resonating Strings** (2015). Her poems and views on poetry and life have been featured on AIR (All India Radio) and FM radio. Nominated for the Best of The Net 2017, she lives in Ludhiana, India. Her forthcoming publications include '**The Lie of the Land: An Anthology of Indian poetry in English**' to be published by Sahitya Akademi, New Delhi.

Time Travellers

Sprawled on the shore of forever
we are the time travellers
talking to each other across
dusks and dawns of tomorrows
toasting our marshmallows
on the bonfires of yesterdays
sipping amnesia we pour into
each other's cups to heal
wounds on our feet that keep
changing shapes of our journeys
like maps we abandoned after a brawl
in the bar that offered us tepid beer
with reheated fish that was beginning to fall apart.
All we wanted to change was the music
but they wouldn't let us anywhere near the jukebox
men with gold chains and Rolex watches
with devotional songs for ringtones
who laughed loudly at the jokes
women in slinky saris whispered in their ears
did not want our songs after they pocketed our coins.

We are the time travellers
forever making beds on crossroads
patting down pockets for stolen kisses at gloaming
eyes fixed on horizons livid with promises
of soft beds and masala tea in glasses
listening to chapattis being slapped on gridles
as jars of mango pickle waited on wall
their mouths covered with mulmul torn from

mother's discarded sari bought from Dhaka
that we wore as children in summer afternoons
when the family took refuge in a single room
cooled by khus padded giant cooler for a nap
and we, playing under the canopy of mango trees,
assumed identities other than our own
took out forbidden toys and invited neighbours
we were not allowed to play with
stole raw mangoes entrusted to our protection
until their tang lacerated our tongues.

We are the time travellers
forever departing and arriving in pieces
held together by long strands of memories
mother rolled and tucked in the cloth pouch
hanging by her mirror, every time
she combed her hair with a sigh
to those places we call home, braving
wind blast in our faces without flinching
with hair so short and sparse that can't be parted
in middle or tied into neat plaits
telling stories of lovers we almost made love to
to lovers we would never make love to
when we grow tired of playing pachisi
with pawns of time held in place under our tongues
knowing there are no winners or losers
other than sap of our imagining, gurgling in
the hollows of our chests, waiting to bloom.
We, the time travellers, sprawl and dream
of glistening shells we broke open
and sweet sorrow of losing innocence
drunk on the apocryphal, on the shore of forever.

collecting apples

Carl Walsh

Carl Walsh is an occasional poet, crossword compiler, lexicographer of fictional words and writer of horoscopes (and other short stories). His work has been published in

n-SCRIBE (www.darebinarts.com.au/programs/n-scribe)
StylusLit (https://styluslit.com)
Cordite Poetry Review (http://cordite.org.au/author/carlwalsh)
Gargouille (http://www.gargouille.com.au)
Cha: an Asian Poetry Journal (www.asiancha.com/content/view/3045/655)
Visible Ink (https://visibleink.net)
Rabbit Poetry (http://rabbitpoetry.com)
the Disappearing (http://disappearing.com.au/poet/carl-walsh)
Southerly (https://southerlyjournal.com.au)
Meniscus (https://www.meniscus.org.au/Vol6Iss2.pdf)

His poem 'Taungurong' was shortlisted for the 2017 Fair Australia Prize.

collecting apples

for Isabelle and Owen

we walk amongst apples	baddow pippin
they decorate the ground	adam's pearmain
in states of decay	dumelow's seedling
the kids roll them over	northern greening
some are rotten	norfolk royal russet
others have a worm	peasgood nonsuch
a few lie on the ground	sutton beauty
in sweet perfection	carmeliter reinette
beneath apple trees	chelmsford wonder
saturated with fruit	kingston black
the children collect them	scarlet crofton
bundling them up	flower of kent
in upturned t-shirts	ashmead's kernel
dropping them again	warner's king
bruising their wholeness	tremlett's bitter
under january sun	tydeman's late orange
their eyes shining	belle de boskoop
deliciously in the moment	nonpareil

Amity Poem

Joyce Parkes

Joyce Parkes is published in *Westerly, Overland, LinQ, The Best Australian Poems UQP, Axon, Meniscus, foam:e, Cuttlefish, Cordite, Meanjin, Landscapes, Creatrix, The Journal of the Australian Irish Heritage Association, Otolith*, and in other literary publications in Australia, Finland, the UK, Germany, Canada, the USA, New Zealand, Northern Ireland, Greece, and the Netherlands.

Amity Poem was first published in *Cuttlefish2*, 2018.

Amity Poem

for I. M. P and J. M. G. P

Is amity a wave
in an ocean
of sentences,
a vessel
carrying sojourns

and solace, a frown
asking tears
to wash the deck
or a sail billowing
on a raft going

from Fremantle
to Rottnest
and back?
I am glad
you and I have met,

sailed, hugged,
walked, played tennis
and chess,
listened to Elgar,
Mahler, Cohen,

and Baez. Shared
a bed, a house,
and have a daughter
who loves and likes
you and I.

Half-sisters

David Lloyd

David Grant Lloyd was born in 1979. He attended the University of Wollongong and received his Masters Degree in 2003. He worked for several years in Sydney before returning to his hometown of Dubbo, where much of his writing is set.

Between January 2018 and June 2019, his poetry has appeared in '*Positive Words*,' published by Rainbow Press. He has also been a regular contributor to '*Poetry Matters*,' specifically in issues 32 – 35. Two recent editions of '*Polestar Writers Journal*' (Tangerine Press) have also published several poems by him. One of his narrative poems appeared in the twenty-ninth edition of '*New Writing*,' published by fourWpress; and another in Deakin University's '*Verandah Volume 33*.' In the sixty-second edition of '*The Write Angle*', some of his poems also appeared.

In February 2019, his lengthy narrative poem 'South Dubbo' received second place in the Reading Performance category of the Banjo Patterson Poetry Festival.

He is currently compiling his first major poetry anthology entitled 'Dubbo Poems.'

Half-sisters

They speak well for three-year-olds
holding hands atop the low stone wall
barefoot and hair-ribboned
swaying their frilly dresses
with their backs to me
watching the garden for lizards and frogs
under the afternoon sun

Elizabeth May sits in the flowerbed
and picks tiny stiff daisies
Chelsea steps over the woodchips
and pats the concrete family statue

They pull away from me and pout
when I try to kiss them goodbye
saying I needed to leave for work
and would not return until tomorrow

from Surplus: An Epic

Janis Butler Holm

Janis Butler Holm, who lives in sunny L.A., has served as Associate Editor for *Wide Angle*, the film journal. Her prose, poems, and performance pieces have appeared in small-press, national, and international magazines. Her plays have been produced in the U.S., Canada, and the U.K.

Selections from her more experimental work are featured in the anthologies *Best American Experimental Writing*, edited by Cole Swensen, and *The &Now Awards 3: The Best Innovative Writing*, edited by Megan Milks. Janis is currently collaborating with other artists on a variety of multimedia projects. (See an absurdist piece on money, here:

http://amp.hofstradrc.org/issues/4-1/sound-poems)

from **Surplus: An Epic**

O how to sing of golden glut, resplendent stuff?
Of booty bright and merry gain, of prizes
shopper-fought and goody bags of gilded puff,
the fruits of orient labour? Comely fluff,
what joyous pealing bell can ring thy virtues great—
thine owner's late heroic heap,
amassed with cost to nature and estate?

Of this, the buyer buying, is my praise.
For as the toys of children do elate, so the loot
of grownups stimulates the sweet pursuit
of ever more, of ever dearer wares,
which greater freight, in turn, keeps turning
all the wheels of finance. Muse, relate
the festal splendor of this paradisal state.

Thinking of you

Alessandra Salisbury

Alessandra Salisbury is a Brazilian creative writer and actress. She lives in Australia with her husband and their daughter Isabella who was the inspiration for Alessandra's first published kids book, **Naughty Nana**. She has just published its sequel named **Naughty Nana and the old House around the corner**, and a third book named **Noise—a collections of short stories and poems.**

Alessandra won third prize in 2016 Fusion Poetry Competition at Australia Southern Cross University with her poem 'Hummus and Herbs' about family of immigrants, and won second prize with the same poem at Wilda Morris Poetry Challenge 2017.

Her works appeared on the American literary magazines, *Anti-Heroin Chic*, *The Borfski Press*, *Seethingograhy*, *Basil O'Flaherty*, *Academy of the Heart and Mind*, *Tiny Spoon*, *Event Horizon*, and *Comstock Review*. In India, she has had poems published in the *OPA Anthology of Contemporary Women's Poetry*. In Australia, her works have appeared in *Northerly Magazine*.

Thinking of you

It's Friday night
around 10:30

I'm reading
Bolton's poem

the one that feels
like 'Talking to You'

he's at his desk
(I'm at mine)

feeling a bit under the weather
despite the full moon

he's drinking the
very last of his bourbon

I don't have a bottle
of bourbon at the moment

but I remember when
you brought me one

the night you decided
to tell me about your fears

when you got me drunk
took me to bed

and fucked me
without taking off

my peach
dress

the one you gave me
for my birthday

in this poem of Bolton's
he talks about

the poems
he might write

and if he will ever get
a bourbon for his birthday again

will I ever get
another dress for my birthday?

I'm thinking of you
now because

after that night
many, many years ago

I only saw you
once more

before you disappeared
at Bill Cunningham corner

Fifth Ave and 57th Street intersection
never felt so empty

where I cried
on my knees

after the argument
you started and then ran off

Thinking of you   *Alessandra Salisbury*

was this
self-pity?

if I asked you
you would say
I was acting

well
I was not

and I had to
pick up my broken pieces

pull them together
and walk away

alone

but why am I
thinking of you?

Queen's CD is playing now
'Love of My Life'

and I remember
we used to listen to

yes 'you hurt me,
you broke my heart'

I remember
Mercury's death

then Bowie's
and Prince's

and the silenced
tune in my voice

our best collection
is dead

Why aren't you
dead?

if you were
dead

I wouldn't be writing
you this poem

I'd be talking to you
by your grave

in my peach
dress

but as you
are still around

I can offer me
the honour

of feeling a little
'intellectual'

and write to you
a poem

I could write
a lot of shit about you

but I want this to sound
like Sunday morning

Thinking of you   *Alessandra Salisbury*

at Central Park
where you shameless

proposed to me
without a ring

and to think of all the rings
you didn't answer

the cries
you didn't care

the words
you didn't listen

well, it's over
long time

and this is
just a poem

I must end it
now

because if
I   leave it

I might ~~delete~~ it later
and I can't

I must find the
last line

are you
thinking of me?

The Nun and the Assassin \
The Assassin and the Nun

C. A. Broadribb

C. A. Broadribb has a Bachelor of Science (Computing) with distinction, an MA in Professional Writing, and a Graduate Diploma in Journalism.

She has been published in a number of anthologies, newspapers, magazines and electronic publications. She also does other work to pay the bills.

If she was to describe herself in three words it would either be 'intelligent, creative and humorous' or 'fat, lazy and tired', depending on how she felt at the time.

She has a number of self-published novels and anthologies available on Amazon, and sometimes sets free download promotions for them. Just search for 'C. A. Broadribb'.

Her website is *www.wildthoughts.com.au*

She lives in Sydney.

This poem won the Innovation category of the Scarlet Stiletto Awards 2009.

The Nun and the Assassin \ The Assassin and the Nun

The Nun and the Assassin

All nuns should be left in peace to live
An anonymous, regimented life in grey stone cells
What sort of future do I have now?

The CCTV images all over the papers
Were embarrassing, but not as shocking as
The irreverent 'Murder? Nun last night' headlines

I had a premonition of disaster at the church that night
Despite the familiarity of it all
My usual rituals failed to comfort me

Looking at the strange woman dressed all in black
Standing there by the altar
I suddenly felt a chill run over me

She was motionless, her eyes blank
The fight was already over, for
There was no hope for an elderly nun

Is a church a place for salvation or damnation?
A brass crucifix fell onto the floor by my feet
As light flashed off metal in the woman's hand

She screamed like someone possessed
Stabbing and slashing in a wild frenzy
Feeling a sudden strength within me, I hit her

Blood ran down her clothes
Wet, shiny rivulets almost like
She'd spilled communion wine on herself

As she staggered away down the aisle
I stared at the black-clad intruder
The door banged against the wall

I crouched in the vestibule, waiting
My heart was pounding wildly
The church was dimly lit, almost inviting burglars

There was a shuffling sound in the distance
A long period of silence, then
The church bells rang out, announcing midnight

As moonlight eerily pierced the clouds
—A sharp, silvery blade sheathed in black—
My good luck charm gave me courage

I called on all my inner strength to face the challenge
Then leapt and clambered over the high brick wall
I stood outside the convent breathing deeply

Having someone's blood on my hands
Was less important than the joy of
Being safe and free in the outside world

The head nun at the convent
Encouraged me to confront and vanquish
The evil that lies in my soul

Being a gentle and peaceful person at heart
Many nights of contemplation stopped me
Feeling like a cold-blooded killer

Read the lines in reverse order for the story of
The Assassin and the Nun

wonderland (in only 4 days)

Olivia De Zilva

Olivia De Zilva (b. 1996) is an emerging South Australian poet and writer who is currently studying her Honours in Creative Writing at The University of Adelaide. Her writing has appeared in *The Adelaide Review*, *The Adelaide Film Festival*, *HybridWorld Adelaide*, *Broadsheet Adelaide*, *SWAMP Creative Writing Journal*, and most recently, the *2019 Poetry d'Amour Anthology* published by WA Poets. In early 2019, she released a short poetry chapbook, **wonderland**, which explores ideas of love and its many mistranslations that occur over time and space.

Olivia currently runs the poetry reading NO WAVE which is held monthly at The Wheatsheaf Hotel. Her writing has also expanded to include visual media, appearing in SA artist, Emmaline Zanelli's 2019 group exhibition Merge which experimented with ideas of collaboration and conversation between female artists. She is currently in her second semester of Honours and intends to pursue a PhD in Creative Writing in the near-present.

wonderland (in only 4 days)

I.

one way to remember you
is by your hands.
those big, textured hands
    tanned and struggling under the weight of a silver chain
clasping a pint of beer.
the first time we met
    i saw your hands and
the chestnut hair swaying against your neck
in the breeze of an aluminium ceiling fan.
our voices
are lost amongst the frequencies of the
    other patrons drinking, flirting, existing
when you say something, i nod my head and laugh
    as the beer on your upper lip coalesces with the
    sweat of this 48 degree thursday night.

II.

meet me at the front of my house
in your beat up old Ford
you've been working all day at the grocery store
    one hand on the steering wheel
the other
outside the window
dancing through the twilight breeze
tell me that story again—

the one where you got lost in New York
with the lead-singer of a 90s rock band.
i want you to prick your finger on my fly—
but it's late now and you have work in the morning.

III.

you're leaving in two days.
i wish you would fold me up into your pocket
and i could live in the holes of your white t-shirt
    that you bought from that punk show you didn't really like.

IV.

i don't like coffee
    or sparkling water
and they taste all the more bitter
when i try to impress you.
i can feel my face contort
    as if i swallowed a lemon.
but it's okay
because it makes you laugh
and your laugh is like that Lou Reed song
    where he talks about drinking Sangria in the park.
you sit opposite me,
    filling out a personality test
at the Scientology centre on Pulteney street.
i don't know if this is what romance should feel like,
    with aliens and Tom Cruise,
but i feel we are connected;
    not by proximity

but by the deplorable results of our tests.
irresponsible, malicious and dangerous.

when you drop me home,
i can see your face swimming in the sunset of monday afternoon.
your big hands on the steering wheel.
i wait on the sidewalk for you to turn around
    to take me with you
    to live forever in the passenger seat of your beat up Ford.
but you are at a red light
    and as it turns green,
i see your car disappear across the junction.

Mr & Mrs Jack-in-the-Box

Dianne Cikusa

Dianne Cikusa has published work in several anthologies, magazines, online journals, and as digital media. She is the author of three books of poetry: **Hope and Substance**, **The Sea In-Between** and **The Rain Sermon: Le Sermon de la Pluie** (a bilingual French-English collection).

Website: *www.mignonpress.com*

Mr & Mrs Jack-in-the-Box

When the babes have packed away
the last of the surprises—

   And the jocks have ceased
   head-hunting in the sand—

      And the matrons are no longer
      dreaming of tropical escapes—

The white flag will have risen inversely,
and the sanctity of performers redirected

'twixt a fleshy bazaar of impromptu actors.

My Dream Mother

Beth Spencer

Beth Spencer writes fiction, poetry, essays and for radio and performance.

Her most recent books of poetry are **Vagabondage** (UWA Publishing) a verse memoir about living in a campervan, **The Party of Life** (Flying Islands) and **Never Too Late** (PressPress).

Awards include The Age Short Story Award, The Dinny O'Hearn Fellowship, runner up for the Steele Rudd Award for **How to Conceive of a Girl** (Vintage/Random House), and winner of the Carmel Bird Digital Literary Award for her **The Age of Fibs** (Spineless Wonders).

Her books are available from the publishers, as ebooks at Amazon, or direct from her website at *www.bethspencer.com*. Or ask for them at your library (thank you!).

You can find her on social media at *www.facebook.com/bethspen*, *www.instagram.com/bethspen*, *www.twitter.com/bethspen*, and listen to interviews and audio versions of her work at *www.youtube.com/bethspencer333* and *www.soundcloud.com/bethspen*.

Connect with her @bethspen on twitter, facebook and instagram, and listen to interviews and audio versions of her work at *www.youtube.com/bethspencer333* and *www.soundcloud.com/bethspen*

She lives and writes on Darkinjung land on the Central Coast, NSW.

My Dream Mother

In a house that no longer exists my mother and I sleep
peacefully back to back in the old double bed.
In the wardrobe, my parents' clothes are careful not to touch.
There is a faint smell of Brylcreem on my father's pillow.
Then the house spreads its wings and flies
over the paddocks. Things rattle out. Safety pins.
My mother's washcloth. Venetian blinds.
The vase I made for her with shells.
My dream mother wakes and yawns.
On a small ornate stool, I sit at the dressing table
with my special-occasion glass of orange lemonade.
The house is dark, and like a good scientist
I fill my mouth and prod my cheeks.
A fury of orange whooshes over the bevelled mirror,
runs down onto the embroidered doilies,
spreads stickily onto the fake fur mat.
I look across at my mother, aghast.
(*"I'm* sorry too" I rehearse the words in my head.)
But she laughs and laughs.
And I laugh too. And the lemonade drips in a glorious baptism.
    & we let the dinner burn and burn.

Ricochet

Bree Alexander

Bree Alexander (also Lika Posamari) writes poetry and more in or between New Delhi and Melbourne. Her current writerly interests include playing with form, multilingual writing and explorations of movement and writing across intercultural experience. Her work has recently appeared with *Enchanting Verses*, *Westerly*, and *Australian Multilingual Writing Project*. She was shortlisted for the Overland Fair Australia Prize 2018 (NTEU category) and she has a poetry chapbook, **The eye as it inhales onions** (in case of emergency press, 2018). She sporadically tweets *@LaBree_A* and blogs at *https://roundlyintheeye.wordpress.com*. Bree is happy to hear from you: *bree.a@icloud.com*

Ricochet

When I dance
binaries into oblivion
and I am no longer
between the walls of
good|bad right|wrong truth|lie
I am but an object
bouncing off
I don't know what
the angst of you
that got inside me?
as I gain momentum
spinning
with the force of me
letting go of you
not knowing
where I'm going to
yet I cannot judge you
even if I want to
parameters long gone
I arrive somewhere
to a place entirely unknown

is it possible to go
so far beyond borders
it was like they were never
there?
to not feel them at all?
but skin newly exposed
sensation on the skin
raising hairs in alarm
aligning with the shift
below
the tectonic plates inside
as a little song emerges
unfamiliar in lyric and tune
and I want to go back
draw lines on complexity
but instead I sit with it
morph with it
become other to myself
excreting a sound
for another birth
within me

There is more

Gavin Mndawe

Dadaist as evidenced by a contribution of a story excerpt titled 'Marina' in Maintenant 13: A Journal of Dada Art and Literature which is curated at the Smithsonian Institute and several museums. Internationally published poet whose anthology was selected for the **Chapbook 2018 Series** (*www.icoe.com.au/2018003.html*). Notable contributor of the KZN Literary Tourism website. A few poems have appeared in the 2019 print-run of Professor Mxolisi Nyezwa's journal **Kotaz**. Mental health activist. Moorish revivalist. Aspiring master faster. Evangelist of the epiphysis. Cyclops. Prince of the royal secret. Modern-day Essene. Owl incarnate. One who breathes like tortoise. Eleven embodied. D.O.B 10 March 1996. Angelo Soliman, Benjamin Banneker and Ziryab all wrapped up in one. Student at the University of eSwatini. Subject of the last absolute monarch in Africa and citizen of the Republic of South Africa.

There is more

Desire
Plus keeping an eye out
Equals what we call
The opposite of fictional.
We only hear a few decibels
Nothing high-pitched, you know.
They talk about molecules
That never really show.

Woe to the puppets
With solid views!
Socialisation is for show.
Anything used to uplift a soul
Can be used to drag it down a hole.

Awareness is structurally studied
By mystics and druggies.
Victimization doesn't exist,
We give ourselves
To the whips and the chains.

I pray for those who are considered crazy,
For there are no definitive tests
In Psychiatry;
A discipline where being shy is a disease.
Crippled with grief?
Having trouble with sleep?
The solution is numbness and drooling.

There is more   Gavin Mndawe

The demented are neglected by the constitution,
The disabled get restrooms,
They get parking
And they live exclusive.

The world is a brain cell
But we're still clueless.
Deep breaths alter the mind,
But they exalt their science,
For the white coat is as divine robes.
In hindsight, I find
Einstein was a Pope.
There's floss;
A fine line between
Brilliance and going so nuts,
You lose all your bolts.

i follow the silent road

banjo weatherald

banjo weatherald is a poet from the adelaide hills. when he's not writing he digs holes, pinches pots and goes canoeing.

i follow the silent road banjo weatherald

i follow the silent road

```
silencessilencessilencessilencessilencessilencessilencessilencessilencessilencessilencessilencessilencessilencessilen
cessilencessilencessilencessilencessilencessilencessilencessilencessilencessilencessilencessilencessilencessilencessi
lencessilencessilencessilencessilencessilencessilencessilencessilencessileNcessilencessilencessilencessilencessilenc
essilencessilencessilencessilencessilencessilencessilencessilencessilencessilencessilencessilencessilencessilencessil
encesslencessilencessilencessilencessilencessilencessilencessilencessilencessilencessilencessilencessilencessilencess
ilencessilencessilencessilencessilencessileNcessilencessilencessilencessilencessilencessilencessileNcessilencessilencessilen

silencessilencessilencessilencessilencessilencessilencessilencessilencessilencessilencessilencessilencessilencessilen
cessilencessilencessilencessilencessilencessilencessilencessilencessilencessilencessilencessilencessilencessilencessi
lencessilencessilencessilencessilencessilencessilencessilencessilencessileNcessilencessilencessilencessilencessilenc
essilencessilencessilencessilencessilencessilencessilencessilencessilencessilencessilencessilencessilencessilencessil
encessilencessilencessilencessilencessilencessilencessilencessilencessilencessilencessilencessilencessilencessilencess
ilencessilencessilencessilencessilencessileNcessilencessilencessilencessilencessilencessilencessileNcessilencessilencessilen
```

it could also be tire tracks. i dunno.

Superseding Professor Weilgart

Chris Reid

Chris Reid is a long time fixture on the Chicago slam poetry scene. Chris is a past winner of the Contemporary American Poetry Prize and has been published in Rhino, Midwest Review, Journal of Modern Poetry and World Order. Chris is currently a student of Arabic Language at the University of Chicago.

Whilst a teenager, the writer was introduced to the linguist referenced in the following poem who was renowned for his work in developing artificial languages.

Superseding Professor Weilgart

I will create a new language
Melding the modern idiom
with relics of ancient human art
It's the perfect solution to the task
of depicting my rebel logic
I should have thought of it years ago

I will create a new language
A pleasant one but not too beautiful
With contexts that tease at meaning
and diphthongs deconstructed
from Indo-European roots
and dabbled Semitic tongues

I will create a new language
Bypassing conventional thinking
use of numerals will be optional
Rather I will employ mystic invocations
to name all colors with a whisper
letting the rainbow breathe at last

I will create a new language
Acolytes faithful to my blog
will disseminate the vocabularies
Over time it will wear easy
as leather gloves but still be
formal enough for Acts of Parliament

I will create a new language
When broadcast to the galaxies
The syllables will shatter into dust
Inhabitants of other worlds
will sift through the afterglow
gleaning symbols they understand

I will create a new language
It will be a lifelong undertaking
As sleep is sacrificed to syntax
each diffident parsing will yield a reward
It will make paper shudder
to receive the weight of every word

to let go

Kelsi Rose

Kelsi Rose has always lived in Pennsylvania, where her words kicked up the dust of country back roads and always smelled of pressed wildflowers and the faded static of dreams. She has proudly published two collections of poetry: **Sparrow** (Winter Goose Publishing, 2016) and **Paperback Wings and Patchwork Eyes** (Winter Goose Publishing, 2018) as well as two chapbooks: **The Drowning Girl** (2018) and **your mother's white-washed words** (JMF Chapbooks, LLC., 2018).

to let go

After 9/11, they stitched patriotism into our spines
and slapped away our fingers when we tried to touch
the incision site. We were only fourth grade nothings,
still malleable, so we learned
to heal around shrapnel splinters
by always expecting that brown hands
      on a bomb

would dismantle us.

Now every year, we observe silence
and candlelight vigils and reinforce the stereotype

that Muslims are all terrorists;
they are still swatting away our fingers
when we try to needle them
under these stitches.

          9/11 is not a surgery I elected to have,

is not a bruise that I need you to keep bumping
against the nightstand; is not scar tissue
for my lover to run his fingers over,
to sigh over, and tell me I'm still
          beautiful.

When I was nine years old, I learned to be afraid
of airplane hijackers, of bombs hidden
under trench coats.

They fed me fear and kept me hungry.
My hands still shake when TSA calls me forward.

I still hesitate before I step onto that plane.
But I cannot continue to let my breath catch
in my throat when the woman in the hijab smiles at me.

I smile back. This war on terror was beaten into us
but I will not break again.

I stand at ground zero, run my scarred fingers
over the names of lives lost; it is a somber exhibit,
where the masses of emotional tourists dab tears
from their eyes with their crumpled tissues

And I try to resist the urge
to rip my spine
from my body.

Perkins Island

Rees Campbell

Rees is passionate about Tasmania; the island she was lucky enough to be born to, and which inspires her writing. In previous lives she's been hippy, farmer, pony breeder, teacher, conservationist, activist, lover and mother. She now writes, promotes Tasmania's wild food, gardens, plays ukulele and lives happily ever after with her husband Col and poodle Darci.

Perkins Island

Where birds are tilted by the wind
carving gaps in the air
and the swell breathes
the tide up and down, in and out

The whales lie still
in the grave they chose
if not the death

On the edge of a lonely land
where the sea is shallow
but the world breathes deep

Where a thousand thousand shells
sprinkle gems
on wind scoured bleak

the whales' white bones
arch and curve
sad and strong
through waves of sand

Rights of the Child

Rhonda W. Rice

Rhonda W Rice was born in Sydney in 1938. She lived in Petersham and Ashfield until settling with her husband and growing family in Green Valley near Liverpool in 1965. She has six children, twelve grandchildren and two great grandchildren. She began writing short stories and poetry as a young child after a prolonged illness. However, she has concentrated on poetry for most of her later life. She has had many poems published in anthologies and has been placed in many Literary Competitions. She has recently self-published her first chapbook **A Mother's Touch** which is a tribute to her mother and has been well received.

Of the poem in this anthology, she writes,

"I wrote this poem for the Year of the Child edition of *Annals Missionary Magazine* to highlight the basic needs of every child.

"The Year of the Child poem, together with a photograph of the Editor's daughter, was so well received that it was used as black and white laminated bookmarks that sold at 20 cents each. Over 38,000 were sold Australia-wide and used as motivational reading for teachers, as well as being read at Christenings and Name-Giving Ceremonies. I believe it still is in use today.

"The poem often began surfacing as 'author unknown' because many people saw, heard and copied the words but not the author's name. It was used by World Vision as the front page of their publication about the plight of Aids children with my poem circled by photographs of suffering children. Unfortunately my name was also omitted there, but when I contacted World Vision they acknowledged me the following month.

"I received a token payment of $25 for the poem and was happy with that. The satisfaction I received from the knowledge that my simple words touched so many people, was payment enough. The proceeds from bookmark sales were donated to the Catholic Missions."

Contact her at *ricey38@optusnet.com.au*

Rights of the Child

Lift me up with hands that hold me steady
I am not strong enough to stand alone,
yet one day I will walk the ways *you* lead me
I am the fruit of seeds that you have sown.

Touch my hand with hands that can be gentle
I am yet weak, but strength has weakness too,
for I have noticed sometimes when you're smiling
you hide big tears that choke, the way mine do.

Love me much for I am ever growing
my soul can dry up just like flowers that die,
feed me with the love of Man and Nature
give me strength, and set my standards high.

Give me Justice, Freedom, and the Future
let my heart and mind stay undefiled,
be my friend and helper while I'm learning,
and—give me Time—for I am but a child.

Rheumatic Pain Stiffens the Spine

Kristian Patruno

Kristian Patruno is an Australian poet whose works have appeared in *Southerly*, *Cordite*, *Rabbit*, and *Westerly* literary journals. Additionally, Kristian's visual poetry was exhibited in POETRY 2017 an exhibition of text-based works that bear a formal relationship to the space they occupy (George Paton Gallery, University of Melbourne Australia).

Rheumatic Pain Stiffens the Spine

Rheumatic:

Nine months for this specialist to define my pain then read me that question of Heroin? or other such histories? On ticking Yes she reshuffled her smile to the bottom of a pile of paperwork (X-rays and CT scans of my character). Like the physio who saw no obvious break but my rocker style, so double checked I was sober
after explaining
my *(Ankylosing Spondylitis, a bi-lateral Pars*
diagnosis *Lesion, and a slip of L-5.)*
and I questioned
like I didn't have English or medical training for "That fuckin' hurts!" while I disappeared up my sleeve as she re-pressed my spine, smiling a little for the intern to see how to check pressure points of a man the hospital spurned last week from its pool, where I'd swam with paraplegics, geriatric hip recoveries, and the nurse who took no time to tell me it's my last session for free; despite how poor health's cost me: my job / my family / and so called friends—who'd not play with the cripple who'd driven to markets their broken legs, or consoled them post abortions.

Pain:

when I evacuated mum from his ice-binge, after he'd skipped a re-custodial hearing. I yelled at my screaming sister who slammed out the door leaving her son without a lift home. Mum, crying poor, ate all my food (yet shoe shopped the city) as my brother surveyed my half reno'd flat decidedly unimpressed with the fact it'd taken pain killers to fix him a coffee then explain my build that the doctors now called rheumatic. plaster chips all over the floors, from blinds I'd half put up to stop an alcoholic neighbour drinking views of me fucking in the kitchen through mirrors she'd hung on Housing Commission walls.

Where her friend died alone, and the neighbour across the way strangled his old-man before punching in her letterbox while cops cuffed him and footy crowds cheered from the street —all the fit young men as heroes when I couldn't roll out of bed to close a window.

Stiffens the Spine:
My new love and her son warmed a comparison. So I no longer needed a blanket to quit all my shit friends. Like the morning the cat died from pissing cancerous blood, I met my parents in Hawthorne Park to likewise put them down —aged 33, the first time seeing them ever sat together— I euthanized my pain by telling them, "don't call or write," in final acceptance that my bones would forever burn from defunct genes and friends. But the important thing is to keep on stretching so sore bones don't incapacitate my re-definitions of muscle or the word 'family' for my kids.

Stove Off—Disease

The stove shocks through my grip
of a handled pot on its burner.
I muse taking my thongs off
to increase the current
option of killing
pain

Health Check

here
in this clinic,
on a questionnaire of health I doodle—
perhaps in better answer than a tick.

Poltergeist Clown

Roger Vickery

I write poetry, fiction, plays, and scripts. Usually I submit to competitions rather than conventional outlets because they're judged 'blind', have shorter decision times and you might get paid for your work.

I've had a good run... 70 plus writing awards, published in Australia, USA, UK, and Ireland and several rewarding co-productions, including an overseas documentary, and two successful plays. Finished works never come easily. Some re-writes take many years. I believe poems should work live. I was the oldest finalist in the 2018 Sydney Slam Poetry Competition which was embarrassing and character building in equal parts.

This poem topped my survivor list because it's a micro story about a survivor told with rhyme (not my usual form), 'real' language, and light touch. The origin point was an image of a woman being haunted by a seedy but engaging old time comedian. The poem seems to work on the page and in front of a microphone. An earlier version won the Australian **W B Yeats Poetry Prize**.

Poltergeist Clown

How can she move on if she's still trapped in his cage?
How can she escape this wisecracking ghost
and start another life, if he won't quit her stage?
If every day is a retro show and he's its eager host?

She was his Girl Friday for so long: seamstress, driver,
caretaker of his clippings—first to clap. It only takes a spark
and that rubbery-faced old larrikin's beside her,
tearing back the curtains and lighting up her personal Luna Park.

Like the time… he split his skin-tight daks playin' Elvis
at the hardware convention. There wasn't a dry eye in the stand
as he nail-gunned the rips and kept workin' the pelvis.
Didn't miss a swivel. Had them then, in the palm of his hand.

She wants to say, "Piss off! All you left was a coward's curtain call
and me bare-headed under the drizzle of all these bills.
Yeah you! Dork on that yellowed poster, bowing from the wall."
But she hard swallows the words, like he did her pills.

"Babe," she remembers him begging. "Get me any gig.
RSL. Bowling club. Any stand up, buck's do, or stag.
But no kids. No blowin' up balloons in a stinky pink clown's wig.
Don't let this business stub me, babe, like a late night smoko drag."

Silly thing was—he was beaut with kids. They love a dag.
And he missed the birthdays when they stopped. "In-dis-creet,"
said the agent. "TicTacs can't hide the booze." He even left a gag
beside the bottle. "Your pills are useless. I'm not even feeling slee—"

Poltergeist Clown   *Roger Vickery*

It's time for him to quit the stage.
She knows she has to close him down.
She's no longer a bird in his funnyman's cage.
She knows she must ex-or-cise her poltergeist clown.
So, she takes up the paper, opens the employment page
and, trembling a little, but ready to grow,
begins searching for any job. Off stage
she can hear his jokes bombing St Peter's Vaudeville Show.

Jesucristo Santifícanos

María J. Estrada

Maria J. Estrada grew up in the desert outside Yuma, Arizona in a barrio comprised of new Mexican immigrants and first-generation Chicanos. She has published poetry, fiction, and essays in *Tempest: The Inner Circle Writers'Group Science Fiction Anthology, 2019*, *Blaze: The Inner Circle Writers' Group Flash Fiction Anthology 2019*, *Spillwords Press*, *Dastaan World Magazine*, *The Inner Circle Writers' Magazine*, and *A Language & Power Reader: Representations of Race in a "Post-Racist" Era*. She lives in Chicago, Illinois.

You can learn more about her other books and writing happenings at *barrioblues.com*.

Twitter: *https://twitter.com/drmariajestrada*

Instagram: *https://www.instagram.com/drmariajestrada/*

Facebook: *http://facebook.com/drmariajestrada/*

Jesucristo Santifícanos

I can hear the eternal mumbling
Of el *Rosario*
In the other room.
I am alone in the living room
With dirty **blue** walls.
More alone than my first day of School,
Where I sat in the aisles
Looking at a woman
I didn't understand
'Cuz she was a *gringa* and
I am a wetback child. I
Hated her and her sick coloured skin.
I hated all the kids who didn't
Know what I was saying. I hated how
They stood up. Looked at the Cloth
With bright **red** and **blue**, put
Their hands over their hearts. They
Mumbled on and on like my *Abuelita,* when
She runs all the words together
From *el Rosario.*

The *gringa's* eyes were full and new.
Not like Your eyes that are
Dying colors.
And You!
You didn't help me! Now, You're
Looking at me with those **blue** eyes
Like all those dumb kids who didn't know

When I said hello.
You know everything, and Theydidn'tknownothing
¡No me mires con esos pinches ojos!
'Cuz You're looking at me like
I'm no good
'Cuz You know my dad's a *mojado* and
I can't mumble the way They do
When They stand
So tall
To pray.

The Everyday Artist and the Everlasting Muse

Michael Leach

Dr. Michael J Leach (@m_jleach) is an Australian poet and writer who enjoys composing poetry across multiple forms and disciplines, particularly the arts and sciences. He is also the Data and Quality Specialist at the Loddon Mallee Integrated Cancer Service, an Expert Advisor at Cancer Australia, and an Adjunct Research Associate at the Monash University School of Rural Health. His qualifications include a Bachelor of Pharmacy, a Graduate Certificate of Science (Applied Statistics), a Certified Health Informatician Australasia (CHIA) certificate, a Master of Biostatistics, and a PhD in Pharmacoepidemiology.

Michael's poetry has been published in literary journals, including *Cordite Poetry Review*, *Meniscus Literary Journal*, *A New Ulster*, and *FIVE:2:ONE*, as well as scientific journals, including *The Mathematical Intelligencer*, the *Medical Journal of Australia*, *Medical Humanities*, and the *British Journal of Medical Practitioners*. Much of his poetry is visual in that the layout of words on the page is intended to be striking, emphatic, and meaningful. He sees poetry as a powerful and flexible vehicle for simultaneously sharing information, emotions, and beauty with others. Michael has given dramatic readings of poetry in front of various audiences at the Bendigo Writers Festival, Write Stuff Bendigo events, Pint of Science, and academic conferences held by Australian Science Communicators, the Australian Centre for Arts & Health, and the Australasian Association of Writing Programs. His poetry has also been exhibited at the Write on the Fringe Festival, the Monash University School of Rural Health, and the inaugural Antarctic Poetry Exhibition.

Examples of Michael's poems may be accessed through his website 'Images of Health' (*https://imagesofhealth.wordpress.com/*) and his LinkedIn page (*https://au.linkedin.com/in/michael-leach2*). He currently resides in his hometown of Bendigo, Australia.

The Everyday Artist and the Everlasting Muse

He builds   a bluestone pedestal for her imminent ascension.
He lights   her sculpted face to give her undivided attention.

He speaks   like an actor from a modern-day television drama.
He creates   a social mask for her piercing eyes to see through.
He plays   improvisational guitar solos, mostly to impress her.
He scribbles   her curves, lines, and angles in A4 lecture books.
He dances   with her guitar-shaped body in all shades of light.
He paints   pretty pictures of her one-of-a-kind psychology.
He makes   her long playlists of his all-time favourite songs.
He folds   her funny origami using napkins at quaint cafes.
He pens   haiku about their reciprocal love on red Post-its.
He writes   her witty texts when circumstances keep them apart.
He composes   short prose in which she is both damsel and heroine.
He spray paints   her star sign on the walls of buildings in Melbourne.
He tags   her in sweet Facebook posts re getaways to London.
He paints   realistic pictures of her unparalleled psychology.
He photographs   her eye-catching beauty in all shades of light.
He scratches   her initials on the walls of caves by the sea.
He draws   her pop culture symbols in homemade lattes.
He types   heartfelt vows for her on his notebook computer.
He speaks   like a thespian from a new age theatrical production.

He rebuilds   her bluestone pedestal years after her ascension.
He sculpts   his muse's face to give her everlasting attention.

The Great Depression

Tim Hawkins

Tim Hawkins lives with his wife and three children in his hometown of Grand Rapids, Michigan, where he works in communications in the health care and biomedical research industry. In his younger days, he worked his way through high school, college and after at a host of jobs including dishwasher, busboy, fry cook, waiter, bartender, landscaper, house painter, door-to-door canvasser, telemarketer, taxi driver, soap factory line worker, Alaskan fish cannery slime-table worker, stevedore, nose-hair clipper model and Taiwan cram school teacher. After graduating from University of Michigan, he worked his way around the world for the better part of two decades, studying the Spanish and Chinese languages and working as a journalist, technical writer, grant writer, adjunct professor and teacher in international schools.

His short fiction, non-fiction and poetry can be found in many print magazines and anthologies including *Blueline*, *Iron Horse Literary Review*, *The Midwest Quarterly*, *Underground Voices: Last Train to Noir City*, *Verse Wisconsin* and others. It can also be found all over the web at online magazines as varied as *Blue Lake Review*, *Eclectica*, *Flash Frontier*, *Health Beat*, *KYSO Flash*, *The Pedestal Magazine*, *Sixfold*, *The Shit Creek Review*, *Tipton Poetry Journal*, *Unbroken Journal*, *Valparaiso Poetry Review*, and *Visitant*. Hawkins has been nominated twice for the Pushcart Prize, as well as for Best of the Net (Sundress Publications) and Best Microfiction and served as preliminary judge for the 47th Annual Dyer-Ives Poetry Competition (2015) judged by Mark Doty.

He has published a poetry collection, **Wanderings at Deadline** (Aldrich Press, 2012), a poetry chapbook, **Jeremiad Johnson** (in case of emergency press, 2019), and a story and poetry chapbook, **Synchronized Swimmers**, (KYSO Flash Press,2019).

Find out more at his website: *www.timhawkinspoetry.com*

The Great Depression

During one of those years
about all I owned
was an old black raincoat,
as thin and cheap
and reeking of smoke
as barroom laughter
in the early afternoon.

Everything I loved
could be carried in the folds
of its dark pockets
where my hands clenched
their fistfuls of roses,
and everything I desired
bloomed there in the pretence
of letting go,

while scarlet petals rained down
and splashed to the floor
along the slick and splattered
length of its blackness.

Meanwhile, everything
I tried to hold onto
pricked shallow, thorny
furrows of resentment,
and everything I learned to accept
took root in the scars

and grew there in secret
along with the mundane seeds
of a throbbing, vestigial heart.

The Great Depression   *Tim Hawkins*

At some point I found out
that when the frozen nights
come early and unexpected
an old raincoat can save your life,
but it can just as easily serve
as your black and tattered funeral shroud,

or fall from you unnoticed,
never to be found.

I never knew finally where I might have misplaced
that god-awful, stinking thing,

but those years took a war to end them.

www.ingramcontent.com/pod-product-compliance
Lightning Source LLC
Chambersburg PA
CBHW030440010526
44118CB00011B/732